Moray eels and cleaner shrimp
live in the brightly colored
world of a coral reef.

Contents

For my mother and father

Photographic Acknowledgments

The photographs are reproduced through the courtesy of William Barss, Oregon Department of Fish and Wildlife; Jane Burton, John Visser/Bruce Coleman, Inc.; Larry Chowning; Department of Marine Fisheries, Dublin, Ireland; David Doubilet; Great Lakes Fishery Commission; John Halton; Ontario Ministry of Natural Resources; S. Rock Levinson, Ph.D., University of Colorado; Marty Snyderman; Daniel Spotts; University of North Carolina Sea Grant Program; and the Zoological Museum of Copenhagen.

Library of Congress Cataloging-in-Publication Data

Halton, Cheryl Mays.
   Those Amazing Eels : Cheryl Mays Halton.
      p.   cm.
   Includes bibliographical references.
   Summary: Discusses the physiology, habitat, history, and past and present uses for the eel.
   ISBN 0-87518-431-6 (lib. bdg.) : $12.95

   1. Eels—Juvenile literature. [1. Eels.]   I. Title.
QL637.9.A5H35   1990
597'.51—dc 20   89-25613
                                                     CIP
                                                       AC

Dillon Press, Inc., 242 Portland Avenue South
Minneapolis, Minnesota 55415

Printed in the United States of America
1 2 3 4 5 6 7 8 9 10 99 98 97 96 95 94 93 92 91 90

THOSE AMAZING

EELS

By Cheryl M. Halton

DILLON PRESS, INC.
Minneapolis, Minnesota 55415

Chapter 1

A Biological Puzzle Solved

Millions of years ago, when dinosaurs roamed the earth, long, snakelike fish slithered through the waters. The dinosaurs died, but relatives of those fish still swim in the oceans and rivers today. We know them as eels.

These fish have fascinated people for thousands of years, possibly because they were so hard to catch and because so little was known about them. In fact, the life cycle of the freshwater eel and the mystery of its breeding grounds was once a famous biological puzzle. Not until this century did a young Danish biologist solve a part of the mystery. Since then, much has been learned about these slimy, slippery creatures. Yet, even today many questions about eels remain unanswered.

6

Eel Families

Scientists divide eels into nineteen families and more than 600 species. Eighteen of those families live only in the oceans. The one family that lives a part of its life in fresh water is called the freshwater eel. Fourteen species of freshwater eels are found around the world. Scientists call them **Anguilla*** eels. They are by far the most numerous eels in the world. Freshwater eels also are the ones most familiar to people because they live in the rivers, lakes, and streams where people fish and swim.

For many years it seemed that eels had no young. Neither eggs nor **larvae**—young forms of animals that do not look like the adult—had ever been found in fresh water where adult eels lived. And no eel that contained visible eggs, sperm, or reproductive organs had ever been captured.

A Mysterious Beginning

Many important thinkers offered ideas about where these eels came from. The Greek philoso-

---

*Words in **bold type** are explained in the glossary at the end of this book.

An Anguilla eel swims among rocks of a shallow river.

pher Aristotle, who lived more than 2,000 years ago, thought eels arose from the mud at the bottom of rivers. Another ancient philosopher believed hair that fell off of a horse's tail into water became long, thin worms that turned into eels. Pliny, a Roman naturalist, thought that adult eels rubbed against rocks, and pieces of skin that came off formed into young eels.

8

For centuries people knew that in the autumn large, brown eels swam downstream from inland rivers and lakes to the ocean. In the spring they saw small, yellow eels swimming upstream from the oceans. But the big brown eels did not return.

In 1856, Johann Kaup, a German naturalist, described a small fish shaped like a willow leaf. It was so **transparent** that it was possible to see through the fish as if it were glass. The fish, about 3 inches (7.5 centimeters) long, had been caught in a net in the Straits of Messina, in the Mediterranean Sea.

This narrow body of water separates the island of Sicily from the mainland of Italy. It forms a high **plateau**, or shelflike area, under the ocean. The strait is bounded on the north and south by very deep waters. Every spring and fall, strong tides surge from each end of the strait. They rush toward the center, where they collide with tremendous force. This action creates an uplifting of water, which brings with it many forms of animal and plant life. These sea creatures and plants normally stay deep in the water or on the bottom of the strait. The little fish caught by Kaup is just one type of animal swept up in large numbers and sometimes even washed onto the beach.

Kaup named this fish, which he thought was a new species never seen before, *Leptocephalus brevirostris.* This Latin scientific name means "thin head, short nose." Although he did not know it, Kaup actually had found an eel larva.

Forty years later, two Italian scientists, Giovanni Battista Grassi and S. Calandruccio, caught more of the leaf-shaped fish in the Straits of Messina. They compared the number of muscle sections that form the back of the larvae to the number of **vertebrae**, or backbones, of full-grown eels. There were 115 in both creatures. The two scientists knew that in other types of larvae, these muscle sections became the backbone of the grown fish. Other body parts matched, too. Grassi and Calandruccio now knew the leaf-shaped fish were eel larvae, but they could not convince other scientists.

10

The Italians decided to study these fish more closely. They placed some in a saltwater aquarium. To their surprise and amazement, they watched as the fish gradually reduced in height, widened, darkened in color, and turned into young eels. Later, they caught many larval forms at sea that were between the two stages. Finally, other scientists believed them when they said that the **leptocephali** (plural of leptocephalus) were eel larvae. People knew then that eels bred in the ocean rather than in the rivers—but where in the ocean?

Solving the Eel Mystery

In 1904, biologist Johannes Schmidt on a Danish research ship was studying fish used as food in northern Europe. In one catch he made near Scotland, he found a leptocephalus. He was surprised and excited because no one had ever reported finding these fish outside the Mediterranean Sea. Later that year, other scientists netted leptocephali off the west coast of Ireland.

Johannes Schmidt (1877-1933), a Danish oceanographer, discovered the breeding place of American and European eels.

Government officials in Denmark and Norway were delighted with these finds. Eel is a favorite food of the Scandinavian people. The officials hoped that by learning more about the eel, they could increase their nations' food supply. Ships and scientists were organized to locate the eel's breeding ground. Johannes Schmidt accepted his government's challenge to lead the effort. At the

12

time, Schmidt was just twenty-seven years old. He did not know how challenging the scientific search would be and how long it would take to complete.

On his first expedition, Schmidt combed the waters of the North Sea, the English Channel, and the Mediterranean Sea. But he found very few eel larvae. Schmidt began to suspect that if the expedition explored the parts of the Atlantic Ocean far from shore, he would find large numbers of the larvae.

However, Schmidt's boat, the *Thor*, was a steamship built for research in waters near land. It could not weather the Atlantic's heavy seas. Schmidt sought help from commercial ships that regularly crossed the ocean. Since these ships were not equipped for research, he gave crew members nets to cast overboard along their routes. He asked the crew to chart the location of each haul and send samples of eel larvae to his laboratory in Denmark. Here scientists plotted each larvae's size and the location where it was found.

The Thor, *a research vessel used by Johannes Schmidt in his search for the eels' breeding ground.*

The charts showed that the larvae increased in number and decreased in size as the ships moved away from the coasts of Europe and North America. In the western Atlantic, huge numbers of the very small fish were found.

Schmidt knew these small larvae were young eels from near the part of the ocean where the eggs had hatched. He made arrangements for himself and several assistants to sail on a commercial schooner that regularly passed through the area. They set off in 1913, aboard the *Margrethe*, a ship bound for the West Indies. All along the route Schmidt cast nets overboard.

Then, just a few days before reaching the West Indies, the *Margrethe* passed through a large area of the Atlantic Ocean called the Sargasso Sea. This deep region of the Atlantic Ocean is roughly the size of the United States. Here the currents that flow from east and west meet and flow slowly in a clockwise direction. The movement of the currents brings masses of yellow-brown rootless **sargassum**, a type of seaweed, to the surface. Small, grapelike pods in the seaweed, which help it float, inspired its name. Christopher Columbus and his crew named it Sargasso after the Portuguese word *sargaco*—which means "little grape."

Here amid the seaweed, Schmidt collected the smallest leptocephali yet found. They measured just one-fourth-inch (less than a centimeter) in length. Schmidt wanted to stay in the area to col-

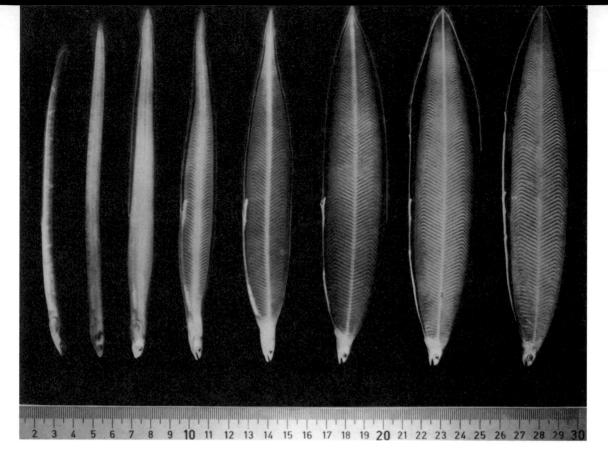

During his years of research, Johannes Schmidt collected eel larvae of various sizes. This photograph shows the metamorphosis, or changing stages of development, of the European eel from larvae (left) to elver (right).

right   left

lect more samples, but the *Margrethe* had to continue its journey. When the ship finally reached the West Indies, it ran aground and sank. The crew and passengers, including Schmidt, survived, and his assistants even saved the eel larvae collections. Yet now the group was stranded far from home without a ship.

After several months in the West Indies, Schmidt and his assistants returned on a ship to Denmark. The Danish scientist began to search for another ship. Then World War I began, and his plans had to be abandoned.

Schmidt, though disappointed, was not discouraged. He continued to study and chart the larvae collections he had. After five long years with no new data or samples, he was able to begin his work in the Sargasso Sea once more. Finally, in 1922, eighteen years of careful research came to an end. Johannes Schmidt proudly announced to the world that the breeding ground of both the European and the American eel had been found in the Sargasso Sea.

Here, under the thick, weedy covering of sargassum, old eels **spawn**, or shed their eggs, and new leaf-shaped fish hatch. The long and varied life cycle of the eel begins once again.

Chapter 2

An Amazing Ocean Voyage

Freshwater eels begin life deep in the ocean where sunlight never reaches. Their spawning grounds are very warm, salty waters that are rich with both plants and animals.

Though they spawn in waters thousands of feet deep, scientists believe that eels shed and fertilize their eggs much closer to the surface. Many billions of eel eggs are released at a depth of 1,200 to 1,500 feet (366 to 457 meters). That area of the ocean still lies far below the surface. In 1,200 feet of water, four Statues of Liberty could be stacked on top of each other. Only a few feet of the upper statue's torch would be above the surface.

Large female eels shed from 5 to 13 million

ball-shaped eggs. Each one is barely as large as a pinhead. The males fertilize the eggs, which are little more than tiny yolks surrounded by drops of oil. Lighter than water, they float upward from the ocean depths.

American and European freshwater eels spawn in the Atlantic's Sargasso Sea. The eels found in Japan, China, and other Asian countries spawn in the Ryuku Trench. This is an area in the Pacific Ocean that is east of Taiwan and south of Japan. Other, lesser known freshwater eels spawn in the ocean near Australia and the islands of Borneo, Java, and Sumatra.

Eel Larvae *(Leptocephali)*

Millions of the tiny eggs are eaten by fish and other sea creatures in the several days before they hatch into the small, transparent, leaf-shaped fish called leptocephali. Having no fins, the larvae cannot swim. They must drift slowly to the edges of the Sargasso Sea and the Ryuku Trench.

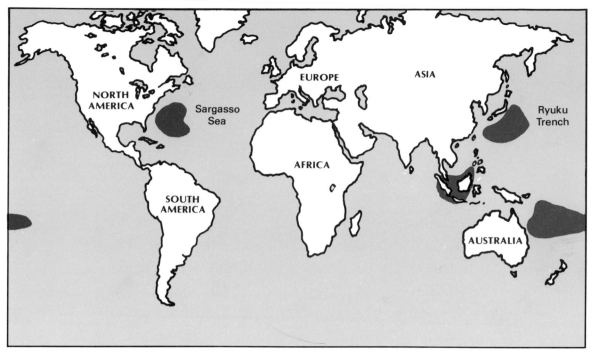

This map shows the breeding places of eels in the Sargasso Sea, the Ryuku Trench, and near Australia and Indonesia.

Unless you look closely at these creatures, you might think they were only specks in the ocean. But with a magnifying glass, you can see they have two dark eyes, and many sharp little teeth. Because these flat larvae are transparent, you can see their heart and a slender cord, the **notochord**, which runs the length of the fish. The notochord will develop into the vertebrae of the eel.

Once the leptocephali reach the edge of the Sargasso Sea and the Ryuku Trench, they are carried in strong ocean currents. In the Atlantic Ocean the current is the Gulf Stream, and in the Pacific Ocean it is the Kuroshio Current. At this stage the eel larvae feed on tiny sea plants and animals called **plankton**. Larger fish, squid, jellyfish, and other creatures feed on the leptocephali. Many others die as they drift into colder water. In fact, of the many billions of eel larvae that hatch each year, most do not survive to adulthood.

The Gulf Stream flows in a gigantic clockwise motion across a vast area of the North Atlantic Ocean. This powerful current sweeps both the American and European eel larvae from the edges of the Sargasso Sea. For about twelve to eighteen months, both types of larvae are carried side by side in the Gulf Stream toward the coast of North America. Then some mysterious force causes the American larvae to separate themselves from their European cousins and head toward the rivers and streams of North America.

For about two more years, the European eel larvae continue to drift in the Gulf Stream in a northeasterly direction. At last, they arrive on the coasts of Europe.

The notochord, heart, and teeth of a leaf-shaped eel larva are shown in this diagram (inset, bottom). In the photograph of an eel larva, the notochord of the transparent, tiny eel is clearly visible.

Notochord

Teeth

Heart

In the Pacific Ocean, the Kuroshio Current pulls the leptocephali toward the shores of Taiwan, Korea, Japan, China, and other Asian lands. They, like the American larvae, take about one year to reach the coastlines of these countries.

Glass Eels

By the time the leptocephali draw near the shallow waters of the coastlines, changes in their appearance begin to take place. They remain transparent, but begin to look like tiny eels. This change in the way they look is called a **metamorphosis**. At this stage they are no longer larvae. Now called **glass eels**, they shorten to about two inches (five centimeters) in length and change from a flat to a rounded shape. They lose their sharp, needlelike teeth and develop fins. The notochord becomes a bony skeleton and adds support to their growing and changing bodies. Because they now have fins, they can swim instead of just floating with the current.

Glass eels begin to use a **swim bladder**, which

The silver-colored swim bladder stands out in the transparent body of this glass eel. The eel's belly is swollen with red worms.

helps them rise near the surface or sink into the depths of the ocean. The hollow bladder allows gases to pass back and forth from the bloodstream. When the swim bladder is full of blood gases, the eels rise. When it is empty, the eels sink. Eels can fill and empty the bladder over and over again, taking advantage of tides and currents. At night the eels swim near the surface, riding the incoming tide toward shore. During the day, they dive down deep in the water to avoid being carried far back out into the ocean.

As glass eels move closer to land, the water becomes less salty. Here fresh water from rivers and streams flows into the bays and inlets and mixes with seawater. This change in the salt content of the water causes more changes in the eels. As they come closer to shore, the eels grow a second set of teeth. Now they can eat plants, insects, worms, fish, and other small creatures.

Glass eels slowly darken and lose their clear, jellylike appearance. They acquire a green, yellow, or brownish color and are now called **elvers** or yellow eels. These three-inch-long creatures look just like a small version of an adult eel.

Elvers can make their skin so slippery that they are almost impossible to hold. This slimy coating of **mucus**—a thick, slippery substance—is very important to eels. It helps them to slide through the water or over rough surfaces easily. It also prevents them from drying out on land, protects them from germs that cause disease, and even aids in the healing of injuries.

While Canadian scientists were tagging eels to track their travels, they made an interesting discovery. To tag the eels, the scientists injected them with an **anesthetic**, a drug that makes them unconscious. While unconscious, the eels were not slimy. Only when they were awake and startled or frightened did they produce mucus.

Elvers remain along the coast in bays and inlets until the waters lower after spring rains. Then, once again, the eels act in a mysterious way that scientists cannot yet explain.

The elvers separate into two groups. Until this time, they have had both male and female traits. Now, those that will become males stay in the harbors and tidal marshes near the coast. The future females move upstream to begin another long journey. This time they will head into the freshwater streams, creeks, and rivers of North America, Europe, and Asia.

Chapter 3

A Fascinating Journey Inland

Night and day during the spring of each year, millions of female elvers head inland along the North American coastline from the Gulf of Mexico to Canada. They travel up rivers and streams as far inland as Kansas, Nebraska, and Minnesota. They are even found in the Great Lakes. In the waters of Great Britain, Europe, and Asia, they do the same.

Elvers travel close to shore in great numbers. People in some areas stand in shallow water and catch them by the dozens in buckets, nets, or cloth bags. Long ago, the English called this pass-ing of elvers each spring the eel-fare. Catching elvers is still popular not only in England, but in France, Spain, the Netherlands, and parts of Asia

Each spring great numbers of elvers swim against the current as they travel up rivers and streams.

28

where eels are considered a tasty treat. Turtles, birds, and some kinds of freshwater fish also eat elvers.

With so many natural enemies at each stage of their development, it is amazing that eels ever complete their long journey. But death alone seems to stop them.

The female elvers grow and darken as their journey continues. They swim through swift, rough currents, over boulders, and under floating debris. If need be, they find a drainage ditch, sewer, or underground stream or spring to get around dams or polluted areas in rivers. Eels can even slither up onto the bank and into moist grass and mud of nearby fields to go around any-thing in their way.

Elvers can live on land for as long as two days, seeking shelter from the drying rays of the sun. They may hide under rocks, haystacks, or fallen logs. Then they continue their overland jour-ney at night. On land, elvers use stored oxygen ab-sorbed from the water. They can also take oxygen

An Anguilla eel will leave the water and travel over land to get around obstacles in the water.

directly from the air through their gills and skin.

In some parts of the world, eel ladders have been built at large dams to help eels on their inland journey. One large eel ladder is located in Ontario, Canada. It is part of the Moses-Saunders hydroelectric dam on the Saint Lawrence River.

The dam is about 400 miles (645 kilometers) inland. By the time eels reach the dam, some have been swimming upriver for three to four years. The trip is slow because the eels must swim against a strong current, and go around smaller dams along the way. Because of the cold and ice, they must also spend the winters burrowed in the mud at the bottom of the river.

Shortly after the Moses-Saunders dam was built, a Canadian biologist saw thousands of eels

Eels enter the Moses-Saunders dam through openings at the base of the dam that lead to the interior wall.

swimming at its base. They were unable to climb over or go around the 31-foot (9-meter)-high wall. The biologist decided to build a rough wooden ladder to assist them. When it was finished, many eels began to go from step to step up and over the wall.

Soon a more permanent wooden ladder was built on the inside wall of the dam. Here the eels climbed in great numbers, especially during the night. A 147-foot (45-meter)-long aluminum ladder was installed in 1980. Since that time, from 1 to 2 million eels each summer have scaled the dam's ladder. When the water is warm, as many as 25,000 eels make the climb each day. Once they pass the dam, they continue upstream, like freshwater eels all over the world.

No one knows how or why a female eel decides to stay in a particular pond, lake, or river. But once the female reaches her goal, she spends years—as many as ten to twenty—inland. During the day, she burrows into the mud and rests. During the night, she searches for food.

North American female eels grow to be about 4 feet (1.2 meters) long and weigh about 3.5 pounds (1.6 kilograms). North American males, and both male and female European eels, are much smaller and lighter than the American females.

About three years after the eels' ocean voyage, they develop small scales in their skin. The growth rings of eel scales, like the growth rings of a tree, can be used by scientists to estimate an eel's age. In warm months when eels feed heavily, wide rings are formed. In cold months, when eels **hibernate**, or sleep for a long time without eating, a narrow ring is produced.

Most female eels live from twelve to twenty-two years, though thirty years is not uncommon. Males have an average life span of ten to fifteen years. One especially long-lived captive eel, named Putte, was caught in Sweden in 1863. She outlived several owners and finally died in a Swedish museum at the estimated age of 88!

Eels climb a ladder at the Moses-Saunders dam.

Chapter 4

Return to the Sea

After many years inland, American and European female eels start to change again for the last time. They are preparing for their final journey. This one will take them back to their spawning ground in the Sargasso Sea.

Changing Bodies

The eels begin to eat tremendous amounts of food, storing it as fat on their bodies. They will live on the stored fat for many months, because once their journey begins, they no longer eat. Their eyes nearly double in size. They also darken in color. The European eel is now called a silver eel and the American a bronze eel because of their changed color.

Other changes occur, too. The eels' snout be-comes less pointed, and their stomach and intes-tine shrink to make room for the eggs forming in-side their bodies. These changes occur slowly. They take nearly a year to complete.

Then, when the fall rains begin to fill the rivers and streams, the females begin their nightly jour-ney toward the ocean. The downstream trip with

An eel swims through shallow river waters on its return journey to its breeding ground in the Sargasso Sea.

the current goes much faster. Within weeks the eels swim from inland lakes, ponds, and streams back to the salty waters near the ocean.

Along the way, many silver eels are caught by European fishermen. These fat, oily eels are the ones that Europeans most like to eat.

The eels that escape the fishermen's nets continue downstream. As they travel, their bodies continue to change so that they can once again live in salt water. Sometimes, the eels do strange things. Great numbers of them may cling together into a big ball and float downriver. No one knows why eels do this or what purpose it serves.

Once the females reach coastal waters, they are met by thousands of male eels. The males have been living in the bays and coves for years. Like the females, they, too, have been changing.

The Final Journey

Together, the male and female eels begin the journey back to the Sargasso Sea. By November, spawning eels have left fresh water and are in the

As eels travel downstream, dozens of them may form a large ball with their bodies. When something startles them, they separate immediately and swim away in all directions.

ocean. They will continue to live off stored fat during the entire trip. But on this journey, unlike their earlier journey as eel larvae, they are strong swimmers. Instead of drifting with the currents, the eels swim deep in the water.

For scientists, the biggest puzzle of all is how migrating eels find their way across thousands of miles of ocean. They go to the exact spot where

they began their life years earlier. Whether or not they go in big groups or singly is still a mystery. The routes they take across the ocean and the depths at which they swim are also unknown.

Are they guided by currents or changes in salt content of the water? Do changes in water temperature help them find their way back, or do they have a secret built-in compass that points them in the right direction? Scientists do not know the answers. But one thing is certain. For thousands and thousands of years, eels have found their way from the Sargasso Sea to fresh water and back again.

After months of travel without eating, the females shed their eggs, and the males fertilize them. Most scientists believe the adult eels, now exhausted and with shrunken digestive systems, die in the depths of the ocean where they were born. Others, however, believe there is a chance that the eels continue to live in the deepest waters of the ocean.

An elver and a mature eel side by side. The eel goes through many changes from the time it swims upstream as an elver to the time it returns to the ocean as an adult.

Chapter 5

Weird and Wonderful Eel Families

Do sea monsters live deep in the oceans? Over the centuries, there have been hundreds of reports from sailors and others who have claimed to see giant sea serpents far out in the oceans. Many of these sightings were probably of large fish, squid, or other sea creatures known to science. Some were probably just tales to entertain friends at home. Still, it is possible that people have actually seen a type of giant eel.

More than 70 percent of the surface of the earth is covered with water. In some places it is more than 6 miles (9.7 kilometers) deep. Yet, even modern researchers in special undersea vessels rarely go more than 4,000 feet (1,200 meters) underwater. Scientists agree that we have

barely begun to explore the ocean depths.

In 1930, Dr. Anton Bruun, a young scientist aboard a Danish research vessel, caught a giant leptocephalus in the southern Atlantic. This strange creature measured more than 6 feet (1.8 meters) in length. Fully grown eels of all species are at least eighteen times their larval size. Because of this find, some scientists say that eel-like creatures more than 100 feet (30.5 meters) in length could live deep in the oceans. They also say, though, that this giant leptocephalus may have failed to change into the adult form of eel. Instead, it may have continued to grow to its full size in the larval stage.

Whether or not giant eels exist, there are many strange eels around the world. The more than 600 species of eels vary greatly in size, color, habits, and many other characteristics. They may live deep in the ocean, or in shallow coastal waters. Some hide from people, while others attack divers who come too near them. Some live in groups, while others stay to themselves.

A moray eel swims on a coral reef in the Sea of Cortez.

Moray Eels

Moray eels are known for their bright colors, large size, and their powerful bites. All have large, sharp teeth. Many have jaws that open wide to allow them to swallow large chunks of food.

Most morays live in shallow coastal waters, especially among coral reefs. During the day they hide in cracks in the reef, in caves, or between rocks. They swim out in the dark to feed on octopuses and many kinds of fish.

A few freshwater morays live in India, Sri Lanka, and parts of Indonesia. In some parts of the world, people eat morays. This can be very dangerous. Some species are highly poisonous, and it is hard to tell safe morays from poisonous ones. Eating them can cause illness and even death.

The largest of all known eels, the giant moray, sometimes reaches 10 feet (3.1 meters) in length. Most giant morays live in shallow salt water near India, China, and Australia. They are also found inland in freshwater rivers.

The leaf-nosed morays around some Pacific islands have outgrowths near their mouths called **barbels**. These look like large, thick whiskers. Three barbels are on the lower lip, and one is on the end of the snout. Leaf-nosed morays have nostrils that take the form of leaves on a stem flaring out near the single barbel on the upper snout. Both the barbels and nostrils are used for smell and touch.

44

Zebra morays live in the Red Sea and near the Philippines. These colorful eels have brown or black stripes on a white or yellow background. Unlike most other morays, they have blunt rather than sharp teeth. They use these to feed on small **crustaceans**, such as shrimp and barnacles, but they especially like crabs.

Scuba divers in many parts of the world enjoy diving in areas that are attractive to morays— warm, clear, fairly shallow waters near coral reefs. In some areas divers are so common that morays have become used to people. Some of these eels even expect to be fed each time people approach. Guides who lead divers to the coral reefs have sometimes encouraged this behavior so divers can photograph the morays. Divers are usually safe as long as they remember that morays can be dangerous and may be frightened by sudden moves or unexpected actions.

Some years ago, near an island off the coast of Venezuela, there was a moray nicknamed Benedict Arnold. It was named for the Revolutionary

A diver feeds a moray in the Caribbean Sea.

War general who betrayed his country. The moray was often fed by divers and learned to swim toward them whether or not food was offered. Eels such as Benedict will rest in divers' hands. But they do still bite, especially if they smell food or mistake a diver's hand for a fish.

Though the moray can be dangerous for both people and fish to be around, one little fish, the wrasse, has no need to be afraid of it. This small fish performs a valuable service for the moray. It cleans and grooms the big eel, sometimes feeding close to its needle-sharp teeth. The wrasse eats worms, fungus, and **parasites**—small animals that live off the moray and that cling to its head, gills, gums, and lips.

Unfortunately for the moray, there is another fish that looks like the wrasse but has entirely different habits. It is the sabre-toothed blenny. Rather than nibbling at parasites while the moray remains still, the blenny takes a bite out of its lip. Then it swims speedily away, leaving the wounded moray behind.

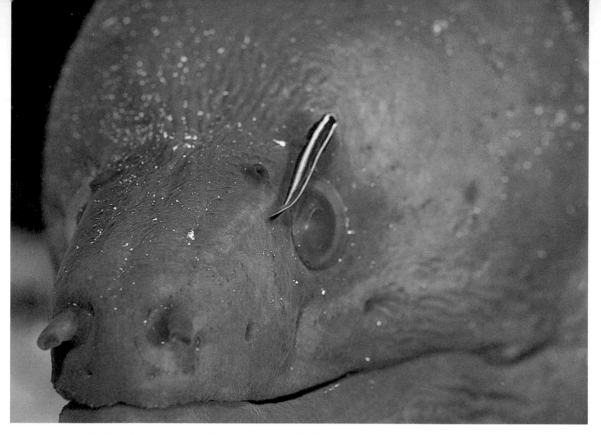

Like the wrasse, the goby is a fish that helps clean the much larger moray eel.

Worm Eels

Small worm eels look almost like earthworms with fins. They have tiny eyes on a long thin head. The largest member of this family is about 3 feet (.9 meters) in length, but most are much smaller. Worm eels live in warm, shallow, tropical waters of the Pacific and Atlantic oceans. They like to bury themselves on the sea bottom in sand, mud, or gravel for protection and a safe place to rest.

48

Conger Eels

Conger eels have long, thin, snakelike bodies. They are found around the world in shallow seas and deep oceans. A few species live in fresh water.

One of the most interesting types of congers is the garden eel, which burrows into the sand at the bottom of many tropical seas. Garden eels are small and slender with enormous eyes and very small nostrils. They rely on sight much more than smell to capture the small animals they eat.

Garden eels live in large colonies in **shoals**, or underwater sandbanks. Each eel makes its own long, thin burrow that goes straight down into the sand. The eel digs the burrow with its tail. A gland in the tail **secretes** slime, which causes the grains of sand in the burrow entrance to stick together. This forms a neat entry that does not collapse each time the eel leaves its burrow.

When it is hungry, the garden eel keeps its tail in the sand with its head and upper body facing into the current in search of food. When a group of the eels is sticking out of the sand, the snakelike creatures look as though they are planted in a garden on the sea bottom.

When startled, the garden eel's whole body retreats into its burrow. To protect itself, it closes the burrow's entrance with a mucus plug. This probably keeps **predators** from digging the eel out of its hole and eating it.

Hungry garden eels rise up from the ocean bottom in the Red Sea as a scuba diver swims nearby.

Slime Eels

Slime eels are fat and very, very slimy. They are parasites that feed on larger fish, which they attack and bite with their rounded mouths. Slime eels use their strong, rough tongues to eat the flesh of other fish. Fishermen often are disgusted to find slime eels dripping sheets of mucus as they are hauled from the water attached to halibut or other fish they have caught.

For the slime eel, the slippery, slimy coating is a means of protection. It is likely to taste badly to any fish that might try to attack the eel.

Gulper Eels

Gulper eels are strange, ugly creatures that live deep in the oceans where light never penetrates. They can be found at depths of more than 5 miles (8 kilometers) where the water is cold and few animals live. Here it helps to have a mouth that opens wide in order to capture any meal that comes along. Gulper eels, sometimes described as inky black floating bags of skin, can grow as long as 6 feet (1.8 meters). They expand and stretch to hold sea creatures of different sizes and shapes. They can even swallow animals as large as themselves. Sometimes, the gulper's skin is stretched so tightly over its **prey** that the shape of the creature inside it is visible from the outside.

In the velvety darkness of the ocean depths, the only light is **bioluminescence**—light produced by the animals that live there. Some types of fish, such as gulper eels, produce light to attract prey. Gulpers have **luminescent** areas that light up their lower jaw and the end of their tail. These areas flash or glow. The deep-sea eels sometimes bring their long tail around near their mouth to lure prey within gulping range.

Gulpers have another remarkable ability—they can tie themselves into knots. No one is sure why they do this. Some scientists think they can force an unwanted object or food out of their body this way or slip from the grasp of a predator trying to swallow them. Others believe it happens purely by accident.

Little Known Eels

Although many more types of eels live in the world's oceans, little is known about most of them. There are brightly colored duck-billed eels, and cut throat eels with *V*-shaped gills beneath their throat that give them their name. Flimsy looking ribbon eels swim in the south Atlantic. False morays burrow into sand along the coast-lines of tropical oceans. Many deep-sea eels are rarely seen.

There are so many different types of eels that it is often difficult for even trained observers to distinguish among them. Yet eel watchers must face an even greater problem. Other types of fish are long and thin like eels, but are not true eels. In some cases they are even commonly called eels.

Chapter 6

Eel-Like Fish

Simply because a fish is long, thin, and snakelike, does not mean it is an eel. Eel-like fish look much like eels, but they are different in important ways. Some have no backbones. Others have no jaws, just an opening for a mouth. Some eel-like fish have forked tails, large scales, or spines instead of fins.

Electric Eels

Electric eels are so eel-like they even bear the name *eel*, but are not true eels. Instead, they are related to catfish and carp. Electric eels produce more electricity than any other living creature. In fact, large ones have a charge powerful enough to disable a cow.

Electric eels are not found in North America, although some are kept in laboratories or displayed in large aquariums so that people may study and observe them. However, they are commonly found in the tropical lakes and rivers of South America. There, people respect the power of electric eels and do not swim or wade in waters in which these eels live.

Electric eels are not the only kind of electric fish. Others, as knifefishes, star-gazers, and rays, also use electricity to find and capture prey, to defend themselves, to navigate, and to communicate. These fish not only send electric signals, they receive them through organs that act as electrical receptors.

All creatures produce an electrical field. However, most animals produce an extremely weak electrical charge. But in water, which is a good conductor of electricity, the charge flows out from the source in all directions. The farther the charge is from the source, the weaker it gets until it finally fades away. If the electrical field could be seen, it

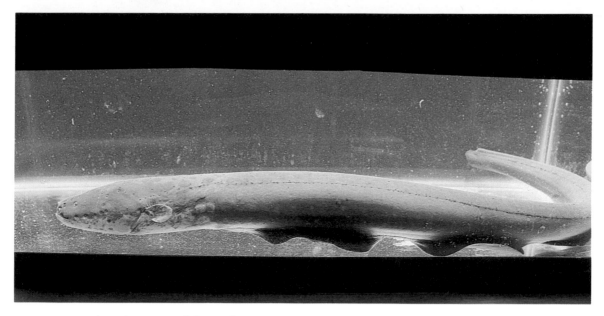

An electric eel has electric organs powerful enough to stun a large animal or person.

would look much like the ripples that travel quickly out from a pebble thrown into a pool of water.

Electric eels produce a much stronger electrical field than other animals. They have three pairs of electric organs on the sides of their bodies. The largest runs almost the entire length of the fish, and beneath it lie the smaller organs. These organs are made up of many parts called **electroplaques**, which are similar to muscle cells.

Electroplaques each give off a small charge. Adult electric eels, which often reach 8 feet (2.4 meters) in length, have thousands of electroplaques. Working together, these cells can produce as many as 350 to 650 volts of electricity. That is enough to turn on a light bulb or stun a large animal or person who gets too close. Each time the fish sends out a shock, it does so in three to five short bursts. It can send such bursts at the rate of forty times per second.

Electric eels can turn their electric organs on or off at will. The largest pair of organs produces strong shocks that stun or kill prey. The smallest pair of electric organs lies in the tip of the fish's tail and is used for **electrolocation**. It sends out weaker electrical charges that help the fish find prey, or navigate.

When the charge is sent out, it travels evenly through the water like a ripple. If the charge hits an object, the ripple is broken up and changed. This change in the even flow of the ripples is detected by the electric eel's receptor organs. The change in signal tells the fish how far away the object is, how large it is, and whether or not the object is a living creature.

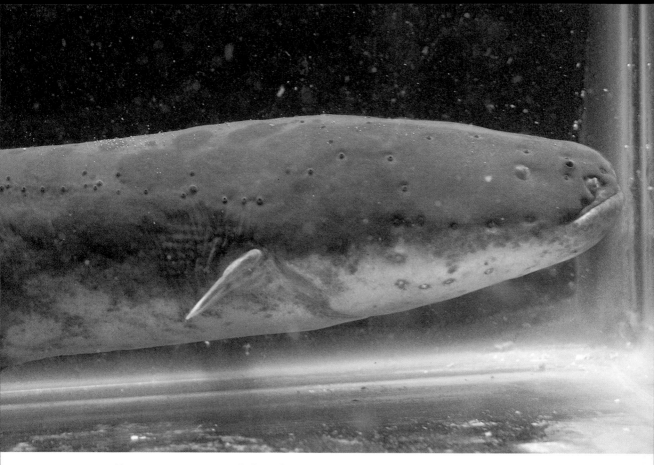

Receptor organs of the electric eel can be seen in this close-up view of its head.

If the electric eel recognizes the object as a tasty treat, it uses its large electric organs to send out a powerful charge to stun or kill the prey. If it recognizes the object as merely a large rock, log, or something similar, it simply swims around it.

One of the first people to study electric eels was a German scientist, Baron Alexander von Humboldt. He spent five years exploring and studying the natural history of South America during the early 1800s.

Before he went to South America, von Humboldt had heard about electric eels. Because of his interest in electricity, he wanted to see them while traveling there.

Once he arrived, though, he could not persuade the local people, even when offered a reward, to catch any electric eels for him. They knew the creature's powerful charge. Finally, von Humboldt found a group of people who agreed to show him a pond that contained electric eels. Here they drove nearly thirty horses and mules into the water, where they were repeatedly shocked by the fish. By the time the electric eels had released all their electrical energy, the horses and mules were severely disabled. Then the local residents were able to catch the fish for von Humboldt without being harmed.

Baron von Humboldt wanted not only to see the electric eels, but to know what the shock from one felt like. He placed his feet on top of a large fish. Later, he described that experience: "I was affected during the rest of the day with a violent pain in the knees and in almost every joint."

Fortunately, von Humboldt's observations of electric eels yielded more than sore knees. He believed that the eel produced powerful shocks when electricity was sent from nerves to muscle. Von Humboldt thought that in humans, muscles might also be placed in motion by very small amounts of electricity flowing from nerves. Though he was unable to prove his theory, today we know he was right. His work has been important to scientists and medical researchers who study how the human body works.

Even today, researchers continue to study electric eels and other electric fish. Dr. S. Rock Levinson, at the University of Colorado Medical School, says that electric eels produce electricity just as humans do. However, they produce it in much greater amounts. He and other scientists study electric eels to gain a better understanding of how human muscle cells work. This information could help them develop better anesthetics for use in surgery and pain control. It could also lead to better treatments for diseases such as multiple sclerosis and muscular dystrophy.

Other researchers, such as Dr. Harold Zakon at the University of Texas, study the electric organs of fish for different reasons. They want to learn more about how **hormones** interact with the human brain to change behavior. Hormones are substances made by the body to help it grow or work properly.

These researchers also study some electric fishes, including electric eels, that have the ability to **regenerate**, or regrow, their tail when it is cut off or damaged. When these fish regrow their tail, they also regrow their electric organs and cells used to detect and send electrical signals. These cells are similar to hair cells in human ears that are necessary for hearing. Scientists hope that what they learn from electric fish may one day lead to ways of regrowing damaged hair cells in human ears.

Dr. Harold Zakon of the University of Texas places an amplifier in water with a knifefish. The electrical charges it produces are picked up by the amplifier and shown on an oscilloscope screen.

Lampreys

Lampreys, sometimes called "Draculas of the Deep," are considered troublemakers by people in the fishing industry. Both ocean-dwelling lampreys and freshwater species attack fish that commercial fishermen depend on for their livelihood.

Lampreys are living relatives of fish that lived

more than 400 million years ago. They are jaw-less and have no bony skeleton. Instead, they have a backbone-like structure made of **cartilage**, a flexible tissue less rigid than bone. Their mouths are round with many rows of short, tightly spaced teeth.

Lampreys attack other fish by biting through their scales and skin. Then lampreys use the powerful suction of their mouth to withdraw blood and other body fluids. Their saliva contains a substance that prevents their host's blood from clotting and keeps it flowing into the lamprey's mouth. Sometimes this process kills the fish. If not, it weakens the host so that it is easy prey for other types of fish.

Lampreys not only kill fish, but according to ancient historians, they killed people, too. Legend tells of a wealthy Roman who had a large fish pond in which he kept giant lampreys. When his slaves annoyed him, he would feed the slaves to the big fish.

Lampreys have also been eaten by people.

A close-up view of the mouth of a sea lamprey.

Julius Caesar is said to have served 6,000 lampreys at one dinner. Two English kings, Henry I and John, enjoyed lampreys so much that they are reported to have died from eating too many of the fish. King Charles V of Spain is said to have suffered the same fate.

More recently, lampreys have caused tremendous destruction to fish in the Great Lakes. The fish entered the lakes through canals connecting the inland lakes to the ocean. From the time the canals were opened in the 1820s, the lampreys took nearly a century to travel from the Atlantic Ocean to the Great Lakes. Once there, they began to multiply. By 1961, they had nearly destroyed the lakes' commercial trout fishing.

The people living around the Great Lakes carried out a plan to get rid of the lampreys. Electrical fences were placed underwater to block their passage upstream. They were then trapped and destroyed. A poison harmless to other fish was also placed in the water where lampreys spawned. This killed most of the lamprey larvae. By the late 1960s, trout were again thriving in the Great Lakes.

Hagfish

Hagfish are marine animals often found in cold waters of the Atlantic and Pacific oceans. They are strange creatures that have a shape similar to eels. Unlike eels, though, they have four hearts, one nostril, no jaws or stomach, and teeth on their tongue.

Like some types of parasitic eels, hagfish produce tremendous amounts of thick, sticky mucus when they are disturbed. If just two hagfish are placed in a bucket half filled with water, it is soon possible to lift out both the fish and water in one slimy clump. Sometimes hagfish produce so

At a seafood processing plant in Oregon, hagfish rest in their own mucus.

much mucus that they are unable to breathe and die in their own slime.

Hagfish often attack halibut, angel sharks, cod, and other fish that have been left too long in fish traps. The hagfish burrow into these fish and eat all their soft tissues. When fishermen pull up traps after a hagfish attack, all they are likely to find is a bag of skin with bones inside.

Hagfish and all eel-like fish, like true eels, have long, thin, snakelike bodies. But eel-like fish do not have backbones, jaws, fins, or some other trait that true eels have. These differences are not always easy to see.

Sometimes the common names of fish add to the confusion. Electric eels are not true eels. And people often call hagfish slime eels, though there are true eels that are also commonly called slime eels.

People who fish for freshwater eels have a different problem. They have no problem identifying the eels—but catching them is another matter.

Chapter 7

Fishing
for Eels

The saying, "slippery as an eel," is used most often to describe someone or something hard to catch or hold. Most likely the saying started because eels are nearly impossible to hang on to for long. Not only are they slimy, they are wiggly and flexible, too. No matter how hard a person tries to grasp them, the slimy creatures manage to slip free.

Eels also escape from typical fishing gear. As a result, more kinds of catching tools have been developed for eels than for any other type of fish. Special spears, hooks, cages, boxes, nets, arrangements of nets, and even underwater fences have been used to trap eels. Some of these have been used for a very long time.

Eel traps at Lac du Grand Lieu, France. Note the wide base of the traps. Eels swim into the wide opening, and then cannot escape.

Spears

Spearing is one of the oldest methods of eel fishing still used. Eel spears, made from the leg bone of deer, have been found that are nearly 10,000 years old. They are similar to metal spears still used in Europe today. Many sizes and shapes of spears have been designed for catching eels. Some have a single blade. Others have several prongs, spring-loaded clamps, or sharp-toothed combs similar to garden rakes.

Spearing eels takes skill and practice. Today, it is done mainly by sport fishermen, because the daily spear catch rarely is as large as that from other forms of eel fishing.

Hooks and Lines

Another early method of eel fishing, and one still used, is the baited line. This can be simply a hook on a piece of string. It can also be a long-line, which consists of a main line with many smaller lines attached to it. Each smaller line has a hook.

Some professional fishermen in Europe and in North America still use the long-line regularly. They string the line with bait, usually earthworms, small fish, or pieces of crab. Then they check the line each morning and evening to remove the eels that are caught and rebait each hook. Many types of hooks are used—flat hooks, barbed hooks, hooks with long shanks, and some with long, thin points.

Traps

Because eels like to burrow or seek some sort of shelter during the day, they can often be lured into traps with bait. They are attracted by both the smell of food and the chance to be in an enclosed space while they rest.

The most common form of eel trap is shaped like a bottle or a barrel with a funnel-shaped opening. The eel enters the wide end of the funnel. But to reach the bait, it must push through a narrow but flexible material at the end of the funnel. When this closes as the eel pushes through, the eel is trapped inside. These types of traps have been used everywhere eels are found. Many different materials—wicker, wood, plastic, cloth, and netting—have been used to make them.

Various types of traps, such as eel pots, boxes, and baskets, are used today in many parts of the world. One of these areas is the Atlantic coast of the United States. There, fishermen trap eels and export them to the European and Asian markets.

In recent years, so many fishermen have

Along the Atlantic coast of the United States, an eel fisherman empties an eel trap. One eel fisherman in Virginia reports that he caught 900 pounds (408 kilograms) of eels in 60 pots when he began fishing in 1979. Now, he catches only about 270 pounds (122 kilograms) of eels in 280 pots each year.

begun fishing for eels in some American rivers that the eel population has decreased rapidly. Eel experts say that the decrease in eels is caused not only by overfishing, but also by the large numbers of elvers being caught. If too many elvers are taken, fewer and fewer will survive, and reach full size. There will be fewer adults to return to the spawning grounds to produce young eels.

These huge eel nets are operated from an aerial ropeway system across the River Shannon in Ireland.

Nets

Nets for catching eels are used in many ways. Sometimes they are placed in rivers, lakes, or estuaries to block the path of eels swimming up or downstream. The nets cause the eels to swim into baited traps. At other times nets are lowered from boats to catch large numbers of migrating eels. Lights or mild electric currents are also used by fishermen to lure eels into nets.

Another way to catch migrating eels as they head downstream is to place nets across bridge footings. Because boats have to be able to pass under bridges as well, nets cannot be strung completely across rivers. Eel fishermen place a series of nets under bridges downstream to catch the eels that escape the upstream nets.

Long-handled dip nets, about the size of a tennis racket, are sometimes used for catching elvers. People stand in shallow water near the river's edge and scoop up the elvers as they swim by.

Over the centuries, the demand for eels steadily increased. Eel fishermen wanted to have more control over the number of eels available to meet the demand. They began to look for new ways to increase the supply. Fishing for eels continued, even as it does today, but the idea of eel farming took root.

Chapter 8

Eel Farming

More than 2,000 years ago, glass eels were caught and kept in holding ponds as special food for the wealthy in Macedonia (now a part of Turkey and Greece). This was not eel farming as we know it today. But it may have been the first step in raising eels for food.

People in Italy, France, and parts of Asia began as early as the 1700s to build ponds to hold eels. They lured migrating eels into channels leading to the ponds. Once they were in the ponds, eels could be kept until they were ready to be harvested.

Not until the early 1900s did eel farming truly flourish. Then, especially in Japan, eel farming began on a large scale. Today, with several thousand

An eel farm in Japan.

eel farms, Japan is still the worldwide center of eel farming. The nearby island of Taiwan is not far behind. Experimental eel farms have been started in parts of Europe and on the east coast of the United States.

Though modern eel farming has been practiced for nearly 100 years, only recently have scientists in Denmark been able to get captive eels

to spawn. Eel farmers must still depend on fishermen to supply them with wild elvers caught as
they migrate inland each spring.

The elvers are usually caught at night with
small dip nets. They must be handled very gently.
Any break in the elvers' skin can lead to infection
and death. Fishermen often catch 25 pounds
(11.3 kilograms) of elvers in one night. When
large numbers of elvers are migrating, they may
net as much as 100 pounds (45.4 kilograms) of
the tiny eels. Depending on their size—most are
about the thickness of a pencil lead—there may
be 2,500 to 2,700 elvers in a pound.

From Elvers to Eels

These elvers are taken directly to eel farms.
There they are placed in warm water tanks with
chemicals to rid them of parasites and protect
them from disease.

The holding tanks are often kept in green-
houses where temperature and water conditions
can be carefully controlled. Even so, it is not un-

usual for as many as half the elvers to die within the first weeks.

In the wild, elvers eat live food, usually small worms or insects. At the eel farms, they have to eat dried fish mixed with powdered milk, soybean meal, or some other high-protein source.

In just a few weeks, some elvers increase ten times in size. Others stay much smaller. Often, eel

Elvers in holding tanks. Some are kept in feeding trays where a special blend of food is available.

farmers separate the sizes into two groups so that the smaller ones have a better chance to feed with less competition from the larger elvers.

When the elvers are about as thick as a pencil, some farmers place them in outdoor ponds. Here they continue to feed and grow for fourteen to sixteen months.

Other farmers have their tanks indoors. With this arrangement, they can grow the eels to market size in just eight months. Eels that are kept indoors do not hibernate during the winter. Since they continue to grow, they can be sent to market much more quickly. Some indoor eel farms in Japan produce as much as 440,000 pounds (almost 200,000 kilograms) of eels per year.

When the eels reach adult size, either indoors or out, they are prepared for shipping. First, they are sorted by size and placed in holding tanks or on sieve trays. These are specially made trays with drain holes on the bottom so that they can be placed under constantly running water. The eels are left on the trays without food for several days

Workers at a Japanese eel farm sort eels by size for shipping.

to empty their digestive tracts and to rid them of extra mucus.

Shipping Eels

Eels, like other fish, spoil quickly when they die. They are shipped to market either live or frozen. Eels can live out of water for several days if they are kept cool and moist. Some eels are sent to market in plastic bags packed with ice and inflated with oxygen. Shipped this way, they are light enough to be transported by planes.

Large numbers of eels are also shipped in specially designed trucks with big tanks. Oxygen is constantly pumped in, and the water is changed every four days. Sometimes eels are shipped overseas this way. The trucks are placed on ships or ferries and transported across the water.

Often it is less expensive to ship eels frozen rather than alive, especially when they must be sent a long distance. When frozen properly and packed well in containers, eels can be stored for as long as six months. Still, the best restaurants in Europe and Asia prefer live eels.

Eating Eels

Methods for cooking and preparing eels vary greatly from country to country. Some people like eels smoked, while others like them fried, boiled, or baked. Jellied eels are sold as a snack in British street stalls. In Japan, eels are often placed on skewers and steamed over a bed of rice. Germans like eel soup. The French like eels cooked with leeks. Some people enjoy eels pickled, marinated, or boiled in red wine. Some like them cooked with a variety of herbs or sauces. Others eat eels raw.

Reasons for eating and not eating eels also vary. In Greece and Italy, eels are traditionally eaten at Christmas. In Japan, they are eaten during the summer. Many Japanese believe that eating eels helps them withstand the heat. For most North Americans, however, the taste of eels remains a mystery, as do many facts about the eel's life and death. Many people in the United States and Canada dislike the eel's snakelike appearance. Others say eels are too fatty and oily. North Americans who do eat them say that eels have a delicate flavor and are high in protein.

A Last Word

Many mysteries about eels remain. Perhaps, one day, some young scientist will, like Johannes

Schmidt, devote his or her life to solving more parts of the eel puzzle. Then we may learn the answers to some of these questions: How do some leptocephali know when to drop out of the Gulf Stream and head for North American waters, while others travel to Europe? What causes male elvers to stay in salty waters while females swim to inland fresh waters? Why do females choose a particular inland lake, pond, or stream to live in for many years? Do eels travel alone or in groups when heading to spawning grounds? How do they find their way thousands of miles across the ocean to their spawning grounds? Do freshwater eels continue to live in the deep ocean waters once they have spawned, or do they die? And are there such creatures as giant eels that could be mistaken for sea serpents?

With all these questions to answer, scientists will continue to study the remarkable eel for many years. Perhaps you will be the scientist who solves some of these eel mysteries!

Appendix A

Building an Eel Pot*

The round pot used for capturing eels is easy to build and lightweight to handle. Eels swim into the pot and are trapped in the bait section, from which they cannot escape. Round pots can be used anywhere eels are likely to be found. This includes bays and estuaries on the East Coast and Gulf Coast of the United States and rivers and streams that flow into these areas. Eels are also found in some inland lakes and ponds.

Materials Needed

> 30-inch by 36-inch piece of 16-gauge, 1/2 inch to 1/4 inch galvanized welded wire mesh (hardware cloth)
> Two pieces of wood, 1/2 inch by 1 inch by 34 inches
> Two pieces of 30-inch-long No. 10 gauge wire (clothesline wire)
> 1-1/2 yards nylon material
> One large bag needle
> No. 8 nylon twine

Stretch the 30- by 36-inch piece of hardware cloth in front of you. To reinforce the ends of the hardware cloth, place the two pieces of clothesline wire parallel to and

*Adapted and reprinted with permission, from *The Case of the Slippery Eel*, by Dr. R. Berg, W. R. Jones, and G. L. Crow, August 1975, A University of North Carolina Sea Grant Program Publication.

1 inch from the 30-inch edges of hardware cloth. Fold the 1-inch edge of the wire mesh over the clothesline wire on both ends.

Roll the reinforced piece of hardware cloth to form a cylinder 34 inches long. Overlap the edges at least 1 inch. Sandwich the overlap by placing one of the pieces of wood (1/2 inch x 1 inch x 34 inches) inside the cylinder, and the other on the outside. Nail the two pieces of wood together. (See helpful hint on bottom of page 85**.) They provide structural strength and form a tight bond at the joint, preventing the eels from escaping.

Outer and Inner Cones and Tail Bag

The outer and inner cones and tail bag are made of nylon cloth (approximately 1-1/2 yards of material). Nylon is a durable material.

Sew the cones as shown in Figure 1, making the wide end about 13 inches across and the narrow end 3 inches wide.

Insert the inner cone first (see Figure 2), placing it about 15 inches from the entrance end of the trap. Using a large bag needle and no. 8 nylon twine, securely stitch

Figure 1. Outer and inner cone construction.

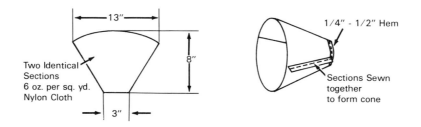

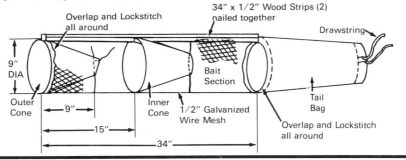

Figure 2. Diagram of round pot.

Overlap and Lockstitch all around

34" x 1/2" Wood Strips (2) nailed together

Drawstring

9" DIA

Outer Cone

Inner Cone

Bait Section

1/2" Galvanized Wire Mesh

Tail Bag

Overlap and Lockstitch all around

9"

15"

34"

the large end of the cone to the inside of the cylinder. Pull the cone taut and tie the small end to the opposite sides of the cylinder, forming a neatly closed slit.

To install the outer cone, lap 1 inch of the large end of the cone over the end of the cylinder and stitch securely to the wire mesh. Tie the narrow end of the outer cone to the cylinder in three places to form a triangular-shaped opening (see Figure 2).

Diagrams showing how to make the tail bag are shown in Figure 3. Secure the tail bag to the other end of the cylinder, double lockstitching all around. The small end of the tail bag is held closed with a tie string or hemmed draw string. Strong, secure stitching is essential, especially in the tail bag where eels are held during transport.

Figure 3. Tail bag construction.

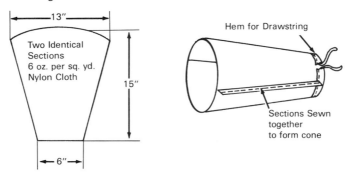

13"

Two Identical Sections 6 oz. per sq. yd. Nylon Cloth

15"

6"

Hem for Drawstring

Sections Sewn together to form cone

**Helpful hint—Here's a convenient way to nail the joint together. Suspend a 40-inch-long 2-inch x 4-inch piece of wood between two horses or chairs. Form the cylinder around the 2-inch x 4-inch piece and place the inside piece of wood (1/2 inch x 1 inch x 34 inches) on the 4-inch edge. Place the overlap on top of the inside piece and position the other piece of wood on the outside of the overlap. Nail the two pieces of wood together.

Appendix B

Eel Recipes*

Baked Eels

    2 pounds of eel, skinned, cut into 2-inch pieces
1/4 cup olive oil
1 clove garlic, coarsely chopped
a pinch of thyme leaves
juice of 1/2 lemon
lemon slices
parsley

      Sprinkle blended salt and pepper over the pieces of eel. Heat the olive oil in a baking dish. Add the garlic and thyme. Place the eel in this hot mixture, squeeze a little lemon juice over it, and bake in a moderate oven (375°F) for 25 to 30 minutes. Garnish with lemon slices and parsley. Serves 6.

Grilled Eels

    eels, cut approximately 2 inches thick
fine bread crumbs
salt

      Skin and clean eels. Roll sliced eel pieces in fine bread crumbs and place on grill over charcoal fire. Salt them as they grill. Serve with a brown sauce with mustard.

*Reprinted with permission, from *The Case of the Slippery Eel*, by Dr. R. Berg, W. R. Jones, and G. L. Crow, August 1975, A University of North Carolina Sea Grant Program Publication.

Appendix C

Eel Families

Scientists divide eels into nineteen families and more than 600 species. The largest group eels belong to is called an order. They form one order and four smaller groups, or suborders. The order, suborders, and eel families within each suborder are given below. The species of eels are the smallest divisions in their scientific classification.

Order *Anguilliformes*
    Suborder *Anguilloidei*
        Family *Anguillidae* (freshwater eels)
        Family *Heterenchelyidae* (burrowing eels)
        Family *Moringuidae* (worm eels)
        Family *Xenocongridae* (false morays)
        Family *Muraenidae* (morays)
        Family *Myrocongridae* (ribbon eels)
    Suborder *Nemichthyoidei*
        Family *Nemichthyidae* (snipe eels)
        Family *Serrivomeridae* (sawtooth snipe eels)
        Family *Cyemidae* (bobtail snipe eels)
    Suborder *Congroidei*
        Family *Congridae* (congers)
        Family *Muraenesocidae* (conger pikes)
        Family *Nettastomatidae* (sorcerers or witch eels)
        Family *Nessorhamphidae* (duckbilled eels)
        Family *Derichthyidae* (neck eels)
        Family *Ophichthidae* (snake eels)
        Family *Macrocephenchelyidae* (rare, deep sea eels)
    Suborder *Synaphobranchidei*
        Family *Synaphobranchidae* (cut throats)
        Family *Simenchelyidae* (parasitic eels)
        Family *Dysommidae* (deep water, scaleless eels)

Glossary

anesthetic (an-ehs-THEHT-ihk)—a drug that causes a loss of feeling or pain in the body

Anguilla (an-GWIHL-uh)—the family of freshwater eels. There are fourteen species of freshwater eels in this family

barbels—thin, finger-shaped outgrowths near the mouth of some fish. Barbels aid some eels in both touch and smell

bioluminescence (BY-oh-loo-muh-NEHS-uhns)—the ability of living things to give off light. Some eels produce light, as do other creatures such as glow-worms and fireflies

cartilage (KAHR-tuh-lihj)—a rubbery tissue found in humans and animals with backbones

crustaceans (kruhs-TAY-shuhns)—animals that have a hard shell and live mostly in water. Crabs, shrimp, barnacles, and lobsters are crustaceans

electrolocation (ih-LEHK-troh-loh-KAY-shuhn)—the ability of fish with electric organs to navigate or find objects in the water. They do this by sending and receiving electrical signals

electroplaques (ih-LEHK-troh-plaks)—large cells similar to muscle cells that produce an electrical charge. They are lined up end to end like batteries in a row. Together they form the electric organs of fish such as electric eels

elvers—young eels that look like adult eels but are much smaller

glass eels—young, transparent eels that look like adult eels but are much smaller

hibernate (HY-buhr-nayt)—to spend a part of the winter in a resting, inactive state, similar to sleeping

hormones (HAWR-mohns)—chemical substances produced in an animal or plant. Hormones are produced in one part of the body, but cause an effect in another part. They act as chemical messengers to help different parts of the body work together

larvae (LAHR-vee)—the early forms of animals or insects that change when they become adults. Caterpillars are larvae of moths

leptocephali (LEHP-toh-seh-FAL-y)—transparent, ribbonlike larvae of eels

luminescent (loo-muh-NEHS-uhnt)—giving off light without using heat

metamorphosis (MEHT-uh-MAWR-fuh-sihs)—a series of changes that occur in shape and function of some animals as they develop from a young form to an adult. Tadpoles become frogs; leptocephali become eels

mucus (MYOO-kuhs)—a slimy, slippery material produced by eels and other animals to moisten and protect areas of the body exposed to the air

notochord (NOHD-uh-kawrd)—a flexible rod of cells that supports the body of the eel larva. It becomes the backbone of the eel

parasites (PAIR-uh-syts)—plants or animals that live in or on another living thing and get food from it without giving anything in return; usually parasites harm and can eventually kill the host

plankton (PLANGK-tuhn)—tiny plants and animals that drift in the waters of oceans, rivers, and lakes

plateau (pla-TOH)—a large, flat area of land that is higher than the surrounding land

predator (PREHD-uh-tuhr)—an animal that lives by hunting other animals for food

prey—an animal that is hunted by another animal for food

regenerate (rih-JEHN-uh-rayt)—the ability of some plants and animals to replace lost or damaged parts by growing new ones

sargassum (sahr-GAS-uhm)—a brown seaweed that grows in the Sargasso Sea and other areas. Little, grapelike pods help it keep afloat

secrete (see-KREET)—to form and give off

shoals—raised areas of ground that are underwater; sandbanks

spawn—to produce eggs

swim bladder—a hollow sac in some fish, including eels. When it is filled or emptied of blood gases, it causes the fish to rise or sink in the water

transparent (trans-PEHR-uhnt)—allowing light to pass through so that things on the other side are easily seen

vertebrae (VUHR-tuh-bray)—small bones that make up the backbone

Bibliography

Books

Berg, D. R., W. R. Jones, and G. L. Crow. *The Case of the Slippery Eel.* University of North Carolina Sea Grant Program, 1975.

Bertin, Leon. *Eels, A Biological Study.* London: Cleaver-Hume Press, 1956.

Friedman, Judi. *The Eel's Strange Journey.* New York: Crowell, 1976.

Halstead, Bruce W., M.D. *Dangerous Marine Animals That Bite, Sting, Shock, are Non-edible.* Centerville, Maryland: Cornell Maritime Press, 1980.

Hendrickson, Robert. *The Ocean Almanac.* Garden City, New York: Doubleday, 1984.

Heuvelmans, Bernard. *In the Wake of Sea-Serpents.* New York: Hill and Wang, 1968.

Jacobs, Francine. *The Freshwater Eel.* New York: William Morrow, 1973.

Jensen, Albert C. *Wildlife of the Oceans.* New York: Harry N. Abrams, 1979.

Moriarty, Christopher. *Eels: A Natural and Unnatural History.* New York: Universe Books, 1978.

Teal, John and Mildred. *The Sargasso Sea.* New York: Little, Brown, 1975.

Tesch, F. W. *The Eel: Biology and Management of Anguillid Eels.* New York: John Wiley & Sons, 1977.

Waters, John F. *The Mysterious Eel.* New York: Hastings House, 1973.

Magazines and Journals

Chowning, Larry S. "Harvesting Chesapeake Eels for the European Market." *National Fisherman* (October 1988):29-32.

De Sylva, Donald P. "The Gulper Eel and its Knotty Problem." *Sea Frontier* (March-April 1986):104-108.

"Fishy Coincidence." *Time* (22 February 1988):53.

Lanken, Dane. "Helping Eels Over the Dam." *Canadian Geographic* (June-July 1985).

Laycock, George. "Travels of the Eel." *Audubon* (March 1986).

Lewin, Roger. "Mitochondrial DNA Tracks Eels' Life Histories." *Science* (25 July 1986):423-424.

Mann, Charles. "Water Pick." *Natural History* (February 1986):102.

"Not Guilty as Charged." *Discover* (March 1989): 12.

Scarr, Dee. "Pet a Moray?" *Sea Frontiers* (July-August 1984):196-203.

Schmidt, Johannes. "The Breeding Places of the Eel." *Annual Report of the Board of Regents of the Smithsonian* (1924):279-317.

Spotts, Daniel. "Eel Farming in Japan." *Oceans* (March-April 1985):30-33.

Interviews

Levinson, S. Rock, M.D. Telephone interview with the author from the University of Colorado Medical School, Denver, Colorado, September 1989.

Moriarty, Christopher. Telephone interview with the author from The Irish Fishery Service, Dublin, Ireland, summer 1989.

Taylor, Joyce. Telephone interview with the author from the University of North Carolina Sea Grant Program, Morehead City, North Carolina, summer 1989.

Zakon, Harold, Ph.D. Interview with the author at the University of Texas, Austin, Texas, September 1989.

Index